The Concrete Jungle Bears No Shade:
Incarcerated Love and Pain

By
Cornell Hurley Jr.

Cadmus Publishing
www.cadmuspublishing.com

Copyright © 2022 Cornell Hurley Jr.

Published by Cadmus Publishing
www.cadmuspublishing.com
Port Angeles, WA

ISBN: 978-1-63751-221-0

All rights reserved. Copyright under Berne Copyright Convention, Universal Copyright Convention, and Pan-American Copyright Convention. No part of this book may be reproduced, stored in a retrieval system, or transmitted in any form, or by any means, electronic, mechanical, photocopying, recording or otherwise, without prior permission of the author.

Poetry's best measured by the depth and lucidity of its artistic perception, by the bold and subtle light it throws and engenders upon the ever upward spiraling struggles of humanity to shake off all oppressive shackles.
Anton Mberi, in Poster, The Roots of Soul 1982

DEDICATION

I would like to dedicate this book to my son Cornell Hurley III; you have been my inspiration to continue going hard, challenging myself every single day, and to simply keep living this all for you. I would like to thank my beautiful mother Shirley Ann Thomas: who has been with me throughout my incarceration whether it be by writing letters or picking up the phone whenever I make those collect calls. I would also like to thank my brother La Christopher Lee and my sister KaNeisha Thomas who both continue to be motivating forces within my life. Last but not least I would like to thank both the Hurley and Cahill families for always standing by my side and supporting me throughout my journey for knowledge of self.

I would also like to thank all of my brothers on the inside who continued to push me to finish up this project when I did not believe in myself. I would like to send a special thanks to Wilbert McIntosh for believing in me when I was lost and had no hope that I'd ever make it out of the concrete jungle. I would have given up on everything if it were not for you; I can never pay you back for guiding me towards the shade when I thought it didn't exist.

Foreword

I have been afforded a great opportunity, and indeed it is a great honor to be able to foreword a piece of magnificent Art of the great .38. What you are about to embark on touches the soul. This body of work speaks to our greatest success yet acknowledges that at times we will miss the mark, but even with that miss we learn to recalibrate, adjust, and take aim to retarget again. And what better way to express life's poetry in motion than a .38.

Life is a series of progressions, we feel fear, safety, heartache, and pains. We feel loss, acceptance, victory, and rejection. Yet our greatest emotion is love. To protect (.38); to defend (.38); to promote peace and justice (.38); to acknowledge that the combination of love (the Black rose) and Balance (the .38) includes the very ability to stand firm in the face of danger yet see the love in growth after the shells hit the ground. To admit your mistakes and have the courage to do better…to BE better…and to continue onward in the face of adversity.

Know that the Black rose is synonymous with growth and love. Black represents the concept of all Lite, all Love, and all Kreation. Fore we can grow beyond our past to blossom into our greater self. We can emerge from the discarded and ejected shells of yesterday to create a legacy for our children, and they for theirs; our future descendants. This is poetry in motion, this is the ebb and flow of life which flows all around us. You may laugh; you may cry, you may contemplate your reality, but most of all, you will see the journey as you read along and understand the drive of not giving up. You will know these things as I have by knowing the great .38. I love you, brother. Thank you for giving us the inspiration and courage to continue and to define our greatest self. Read and enjoy!

The Black Tigon of Jah… (JJR)

Preface

Since my birth I've felt as if I was incarcerated. My life has been far from great. Many opportunities have passed me by due to my lack of knowledge. A majority of my life I was held captive and controlled by fear. After writing my book no longer am I held captive or controlled by fear. No longer does it matter if the world knows that I write from within a cell. Society may feel as though they have taken freedom from me. However, I would like to thank society for the time in which I now serve. It is because of the time I serve incarcerated that I am now free.

CORNELL HURLEY JR.

AFFIDAVIT IN SUPPORT OF SEARCH WARRANT

STATE OF TENNESSEE
COUNTY OF MONTGOMERY

Personally appeared before _____, Judge of the Montgomery County General Sessions Court for said State, the undersigned Detective Michael Ulrey, of the Clarksville Police Department, and now makes oath in due form of law that there is probable and reasonable cause to believe that 2020 Lintwood Drive apartment B, Clarksville TN, and a red 2005 Nissian 350Z bearing TX registration CJT6250, parked at the same address, is now in possession of certain evidence of a crime, to wit: violations of state laws as set forth in TCA Section 39-13-201, Criminal Homicide, and the evidence to be searched for is as follows:

A 9mm firearm, firearm parts, magazines, 9mm ammunition and casings, gunshot residue, clothing worn by Carnell Hurley during the homicide, specifically, a blue or gray long sleeve shirt and dark colored pants.

The Affiant further testifies that the said evidence is now located and may be found in possession of said location located in Montgomery County, Tennessee, and more particularly described as follows: From the intersection of Skyview Circle and Lintwood Drive travel in an Easterly direction for .4 mile on Lintwood Drive. 2020 Lintwood Drive will be located on the right side of the road and is a two story red brick residence with a red shingled roof. The number 2020 is clearly marked with white letters on the front of the residence. The residence is divided into two apartments, apartment A is the right door as you face the structure and apartment B will be the left door. The search shall include all outbuildings, outhouses and storage buildings, and all vehicles found thereon for the aforesaid evidence; and if you find the same, or any part thereof, you shall seize the evidence and safe keep the same in Clarksville, Tennessee, pending further orders of the Criminal Court for Montgomery County, Clarksville TN.

Statement of Facts In Support of Probable Cause

On February 6, 2015, at approximately 11:53 PM, Officers of the Clarksville Police Department responded to a shooting call at The Lodge Sports Pub at 3025 Mr. C Drive in Clarksville TN. When Officers arrived they found that three subjects had been shot, two of the subjects were transported for medical treatment, and the third was deceased. The deceased subject was identified as Terence Harwell.

During the investigation, Cornell HURLEY was developed as a possible suspect, and was identified by a witness as the person who shot Terence Harwell.

During an interview with Cornell HURLEY, he advised that he had been in an altercation in the club and was thrown out. While outside, some guys wanted to continue to fight, HURLEY advised that he retrieved a gun from his vehicle, a red 2005 Nissan 350Z, and fired numerous shots, HURLEY returned to his vehicle and reloaded the gun and fired more rounds. HURLEY then returned to his vehicle and left, driving home.

HURLEY advised that the gun he was shooting is in the glove box of his 2005 Nissan 350Z.

According to police records, HURLEY has a red 2005 Nissan 350Z registered in his name, and the vehicle has Texas registration CJT6250

HURLEY listed 2020 Lintwood Drive apartment B, Clarksville TN as his home address during the interview.

According to records of the Clarksville Department of Electricity, Cornell HURLEY is the account holder at 2020 Lintwood Drive in Clarksville TN.

I Swear the Foregoing is True under Penalty of Perjury.

_____ 6/1/15
AFFIANT

Sworn to and Subscribed before me at 4:08 o'clock PM, on this 7th day of February 2015.

_____
Judge of Part __ of the General Sessions Court of Montgomery County

CORNELL HURLEY JR.

CORRECTED COPY

CONTINUATION SHEET, DD Form 2707-1 – PFC Cornell Hurley, Jr., 428-69-4578, U.S. Army, F Company, 2-320th Field Artillery Regiment, 101st Division Artillery, 101st Airborne Division (Air Assault), Fort Campbell, KY 42223

Item 3 Continued:

3. SUMMARY OF OFFENSES, PLEAS AND FINDINGS continued					
a. CHARGE/SPECIFICATION	b. UCMJ ARTICLE(S)	c. DIBRS CODE	d. BRIEF DESCRIPTION OF OFFENSE	e. PLEA	f. FINDING
Charge I	118		To Charge I	NG	G
The Specification		118-A	Did, at or near Clarksville, Tennessee, on or about 6 February 2015, with premeditation, murder Sergeant T.H. by means of shooting him, with a loaded firearm.	NG	NG^3
Charge II	80		To Charge II	NG	G
Specification 1		118-B-	Did, at or near, Clarksville, Tennessee, on or about 6 February 2015, attempt to murder, with premeditation, Private First Class R.R. by shooting him multiple times with a loaded firearm, causing grievous bodily harm.	NG	NG^4
Specification 2		118-B-	Did, at or near, Clarksville, Tennessee, on or about 6 February 2015, attempt to murder with premeditation, Private First Class D.M. by shooting at him with a loaded firearm.	NG	NG^5
Specification 3		118-B-	Did, at or near Clarksville, Tennessee, on or about 6 February 2015, attempt to murder, with premeditation, Private First Class K. M. by shooting him with a loaded firearm, causing grievous bodily harm.	NG^1	NG^6
Charge III	128			D^2	D^2
The Specification		128-B-	Did, at or near Clarksville, Tennessee, on or about 6 February 2015, unlawfully touch A.W. on her hips and waist with his hands.	D^2	D^2
			(END OF CHARGES)		

NG^1 - After arraignment and prior to entry of pleas, the government made a motion to delete the words "causing grievous bodily harm." There being no objection by the defense, the military judge granted the motion.

D^2 - After arraignment and prior to entry pleas, the trial counsel made a motion to dismiss Charge III and its Specification. There being no objection by the defense, the military judge granted the motion.

NG^3 - Of The Specification of Charge I: Not Guilty, but Guilty of Article 118, Unpremeditated Murder.

NG^4 - Of Specification 1 of Charge II: Not Guilty, but Guilty of Article 128, Aggravated Assault in which Grievous Bodily Harm is Intentionally Inflicted. (DIBRS CODE: 128-J2)

NG^5 - Of Specification 2 of Charge II: Not Guilty, but Guilty of Article 80, Attempted Unpremeditated Murder.

NG^6 - Of Specification 3 of Charge II: Not Guilty, but Guilty of Article 128, Aggravated Assault with a Dangerous Weapon or Other Means or Force Likely to Produce Death or Grievous Bodily Harm. (DIBRS CODE: 128-H2)

If you are looking for a story where the sun rises in the east and sets in the west, which is completely normal, then read no further. However, if you are willing to take a ride on an emotional roller coaster, sit back and enjoy the highs and lows of my life. A life in which I know most people will never understand no matter how many times they read this book. Take a look through my eyes and see things that the average mind could not possibly fathom, family issues, abuse, my culture, and most important, my neighborhood. You should also know that this book was not composed in a quiet place nor a place of comfort. This book was put together in the midst of chaos, violence, and confinement. Unlike most poets I could not place myself in a different environment so that I may alter my mind or mood. With every poem I had to go back to a time when I was once free. Free from daily harassment, brutal attacks, and an environment overpopulated with toxic masculinity. For a brief moment allow me to take you back...

I was born September 6, 1990 in Cleveland, MS and named after my father Cornell Hurley. Growing up in Mississippi was like heaven to me as a child. It was as if the entire world revolved around me. There was always so much to do as a child. In fact, I cannot recall one dull moment. I've heard stories about how people pay thousands of dollars to travel and see what they refer to as the Seven Wonders of the World. Fortunately for me, I did not have to travel, nor did I have to pay a dime to see what most would pay for. One of the Seven Wonders of the World, as far as I am concerned, stood right before me in Mississippi. It was always a beautiful sight to see. As a child I remember waking up before dawn looking beyond my window at the corn fields that seemed to stretch as far as the eyes could see. Once the sun broke the horizon, the corn field would shine brighter than the sun itself, appearing as a land full of gold. Beyond the fields which I dared not enter, everything else was fair game. I could go wherever I wanted to go.

The neighborhood that seemed so big to me as a child was not big at all. To be honest with you, I did not grow up in Cleveland, Mississippi, but just along the outskirts in a small town called Renova. Renova only consisted of about eight streets, mostly made of gravel and dirt. Everyone who lived in Renova knew one another; it was definitely a tight-knit community. It was a trailer park community which did not bother me at all. I thought it was cool that my home had wheels underneath it. I remember desperately wanting my mother to hook our home to a truck so that we could ride cross country as I laid in bed enjoying the view from my window. Honestly, there is no place I would rather be than Renova, Mississippi. I even wrote a poem about Renova in order to show my gratitude to the place which raised me and made me who I am today. I miss my hometown and now that I'm incarcerated I long to go home.

Though the sunshine may have made the corn fields just beyond my window shine like a pot of gold, it could do nothing for the inside of my home. On the inside of my home, it was as if someone had smudged coal along the walls, it was a very dark place. My mother Shirley Ann Thomas, one of the strongest black women I know, did all that she could to repaint the inside of our home. I remember not having my mother around much growing up. My mother would work all kinds of crazy hours so that she could provide for not only myself but my brother and sister as well. My mother and I would spend about 30 minutes each morning with one another before I headed off to school and I wouldn't see her again until it was time for bed that night. Though my mom tried extremely hard to form a connection with me as a child, we just didn't connect. For multiple reasons, as a child I did not like my mother. I now know I was too young to understand all that she was going through. At the time I just felt she could have done more to protect our home. I figured if anyone could remove the smudges from the walls inside our home it was my mother.

Growing up I witnessed things no child should have to see. The biggest issue within my home was that I had no father figure. My father was murdered when I was far too young to remember. I spent time with my father, but I only know of such occasions because of stories I've been told. If my father was not murdered, I am sure that the inside of my home would have looked a lot different. The reality of it all was that I would never have a father and it would affect me for the rest of my life. After my father's death my mother married La Christopher Lee which is my younger brother's father. La Christopher was a hard person to like as a child. He would treat my sister, my brother, and I with the utmost respect. However, when I tightly close my eyes attempting to block out the way he treated my mother, I am unsuccessful every time.

I can still feel the foundation of our trailer home quake beneath my feet. Often I tried to imagine that it was storming outside because the only thing other than my mother receiving a beating that would cause the house to shake was a thunderstorm. My brother and sister would run to me for comfort whenever my mother and Chris would fight. I wanted so badly to cry for my mother, to shout at the top of my lungs for Chris to stop or at the very least go find help. Even though I wanted to help I was always crippled by fear. Fear that I would not dare show in the company of my brother and sister. I would hold the both of them while they cried, and I'd watch my mother be brutally beaten without blinking an eye. To further comfort them I began to make fun of Chris and my mother as they would fight in order to have my brother and sister laugh instead of cry, and when that didn't work, I began to join in on the fights in a desperate attempt to help my mother. Sometimes I was successful at getting my brother and sister to laugh but no matter how hard I fought I could never stop Chris's actions. My mother at times when she was being beaten would call out to me for help. I always felt bad listening to her repeatedly saying my name knowing that I could do nothing to save her.

As I write these words, I still find it hard to express my feelings in the manner in which I truly should. Though many people may not purchase, let alone read this book, I still find it quite hard to be vulnerable. After serving seven years in a maximum security prison, I've become somewhat numb to my emotions. I now know what it feels like to stare in the mirror and truly not recognize the person staring back at you.

I was 25 years old when I was sentenced to 25 years for Unpremeditated Murder, Aggravated Assault in which grievous bodily harm is intentionally inflicted. Attempted Unpremeditated Murder and Aggravated Assault with a dangerous weapon. For the last seven years I've let the charges in which I was convicted decide who I was going to be as a man. Without any guidance on the inside, I walked, talked, thought, and often at times acted as if I was nothing more than a murderer. I was unaware of what I had already lost, so I continued to put myself in situations that caused me to lose more. After spending a few years within solitary confinement, I was still unaware of what I was missing out on. I couldn't see beyond the walls of the concrete jungle which until this very day holds me captive. My wife gave birth to my son Cornell Hurley III while I was incarcerated and though my son means the world to me, not even his birth was enough for me to change my ways. I began to use his birth as a reason to go harder than I ever had before. I prided myself on the thought of knowing that no one would ever be able to tell my son that his father was anything less than a standup guy.

CORNELL HURLEY JR.

    Growing up I decided at an early stage that the last thing I would ever be known as was a pushover. There were no adults around informing me on what I should be doing with my time and energy as a child, which I do not use as an excuse. However, the streets let it be known that to be anything less than a standup guy was unacceptable. Needless to say, growing up in the streets caused me to display every single characteristic trait of toxic masculinity. Even as I write these words I still find it hard to display any emotion other than anger. I guess you can say that I am still a work in progress.

    So, the question is: What can a person who sincerely wants to change their life do about it once incarcerated? Some may say that it's too late for change once you've entered prison or that rehabilitation is merely impossible while on the inside. Anyone who thinks such a thing could not be any further from the truth. Within the last few years alone I've begun to make drastic changes in the way in which I conduct myself, without the help of my confining facility's rehabilitation programs. How? By simply picking up my pen and pad, whether it be a journal entry or a poem. I've found joy in allowing my emotions to be expressed in a nontoxic manner. Expressing myself in this manner has allowed for me to be honest with myself and to find out who I truly am. I would advise anyone who may be sitting inside a cell or anyone who is on the outside but continues to find themselves confined by their day-to-day issues to pick up a pen and get to writing. By no means necessary am I saying that you must write a book, but you must at some point begin to have more than a surface relationship with yourself, which can be done by writing.

    Though I am not yet mentioned when people speak of New York Times bestselling authors, I can assure that one day I will be. Even though I am confined in a level-five facility and have had most of my rights taken away, I refuse to allow my voice to be muffled. I will be heard. I can assure you that though this is my first book, it will not be my last. I know that my words are meaningful and will have a great impact on the world.

    I believe in you just as much as I believe in myself. Writing a book wasn't the easiest thing to do but the journey was worthwhile. If I can do this from the confinement of my cell, imagine what you can do if only you tried hard enough.

    Much love,

THE CONCRETE JUNGLE BEARS NO SHADE

The greatest weapon that the oppressor has in his hand is the mind of the oppressed.
    Ibid

The flowers take tears/of the weeping night/and give them to the sun/for the day's delight.
    Joseph S. Cotter, Sr., c. 1900

Black Rose Down

How am I to rise
How am I to survive
When smothered by oppressors
Who feel the need to beat me down
So that they may survive
I get little to no sunlight
As my oppressors surround me
All I see is a cotton white sky
Sunshine can't reach beyond the crowds
That gather around watching me be beaten down.
In the darkest spot in darkness I hide
Doing my best to stay away
Praying for sunshine without a single cloud in mind
Waiting on its rays to bless my flesh
Which I know won't last long
Before a group of clouds come along again
To steal my joy and beat me down
That'll be one less black flower around
How my heart mourns
For black roses smothered by clouds
Who decided our fate
Knocking us to the ground
I long for the day I will no longer see
Another Black Rose Down.

CORNELL HURLEY JR.

The start of weeping is hard.
    Africa

Would it please you if I strung my tears/in pearls for you to wear.
    Neomi Madgett, The Race Question, Star by Star 1965

Black Tears

Does my black complexion camouflage my black tears
So my cries only reach those with deaf ears
On my knees at night
Maybe I'm not praying right
As I cry my black tears
With the history of my folks
Being used and abused they think it's merely impossible
For me to shed these black tears
Looking at the bible
They only show pictures of white angels
So they think it's impossible for us to fly
Yet alone shed these black tears.
Well as long as I'm Black
And continue to cry these black tears of mine
Believe me when I say you have no reason to fear
I've traveled an unpaved path crying black tears of tar
While on my way to joy
So travel down the straight path if you will
Once you reach a dead end
There you will find me at a place where we no longer shed black tears.

CORNELL HURLEY JR.

The heart of man is a gift of God. Beware of neglecting it.
    Egypt

The heart is not a knee that can be bent.
    Senegal

SAFE

I've learned not to do it so hard
To stand up and not fall when confronted with it
Run away when it begins to give chase
Because of you I'm sliding across home plate heart in hand
It's because of you I'm playing it safe
And may never love again.

Friendship takes fear from the heart.
    Mahabharata 5-1 B.C.

Being a friend means mastering the art of timing. There is a time for silence. A time to let go and allow people to hurl themselves into their own history. And a time to pick up the pieces when it's all over.
    Gloria Naylor, The Women of Brewster Place 1988

It's You and Me

This can't be you and I
You and I, us we can't be
I know all there is to know about you
You know all there is to know about me
Our connection is concrete so how could we be
I want you in the same way, you want me
So friends you and I, we can't be.

CORNELL HURLEY JR.

All things in the universe move in cycles; so who knows but that in the whirl of God's great wheel the torch may again flame in the upper valley of the Nile.
    James Weldon Johnson 1919

SHINING STAR

The other night I laid awake
With my eyes fixed to the ceiling
While captivating thoughts of you clouded my mind
I could only think of you as I rose to my feet adoring the night sky
I wondered if you might be doing the same
As I gazed beyond my window I was amazed
I imagined you were the brightest star of the night
Even after the sky became somewhat cloudy and grey
And the morning light began to shine
You still shined bright enough to be seen through it all
No birds, clouds, or planes will do
Because now when I look towards the heavens
I'm only looking for you
Shining star you have my heart
And no matter where I go
I will always know exactly where you are
Because you my love are my one and only
Shining star

He who asks questions cannot avoid answers.
    Cameroon

Question everything. Every stripe, every star, every word spoken. Question everything.
    Ernest Gaines 1968

QUESTION

Where is it I need look
Where is it I need to be
What is it and where could it be
Why is it I find myself seeking
Why is it that it doesn't find me
How is it I want it so bad
How is it that I want it when it never lasts
When will you come to me or will you ever
Because I've yet to have love
I have no answer to any of the questions above.

CORNELL HURLEY JR.

If the dance is pleasing, even the lame will crawl to it.
    Africa

He who cannot dance will say: The drum is bad.
    Africa

FEELING FINE

I got a tune in mind
That'll make the birds sing along
I got a pep in my step
That'll make the lame rise
I have a few dollars in my pocket
Not enough for my hopes and dreams
But everything is going to be fine
I'm fine with this here life of mine
You see I got that tune of mine
That pep in my step
A few dollars short of a check
I'd say I'm doing just fine
So do me a favor
Don't worry 'bout me and mine
Because if you ask
I'll be glad to tell you
That I'm doing mighty fine

CORNELL HURLEY JR.

THE CONCRETE JUNGLE BEARS NO SHADE

CORNELL HURLEY JR.

A little pool with water! Yet men drown in it.
    Niger

It's like living in a flower garden, you might pluck one, but that doesn't mean you remember it.
    Eubie Blake, Eubie 1979

Deep Conversation

Got a mouth full of words to say
Allow me to spell 'em out
So that you can feel every word I say
This conversation won't be held face to face
I wanna hold court between your waist
With the tip of my tongue
I'm applying pressure
Tongue tied I speak different languages to the box
She looking down amazed at what I say
Looking up I can see your face
Feel a slight tingle between your waist
Love when you arch your back
Bringing it closer to my face
Now I know that you're listening carefully to what I said
Running out of words
Got to come up
Time to take a break
Gripping the back of your neck
Now we really face to face
Tongue kissing, fingers between your legs
Hope every word I said was heart felt
Because if you didn't feel it
Let me know and I'll start from the top
Because the conversation is never truly done
There is always so much more to say
But trust me this conversation won't be face to face.

CORNELL HURLEY JR.

My writing was more an attempt at understanding self than self-expression.
    Richard Wright, in America Mercury, July 1961

Writing really helps you heal yourself.
    Alice Walker, c. 1983

Treasured

You've found my treasures and studied them day and night
You've shared them with your close friends
And in front of large crowds you've read them aloud
My deepest thoughts, my secrets, and past experiences
Are now exposed because of you
My treasures are to last longer than gold
When I'm old and grey
The story of my treasures will continue to be told
Sweeter than honey much purer than gold
My treasures shall live on after I'm dead and gone

CORNELL HURLEY JR.

Everyone is more or less the master of his own fate.
        Aesop, "The Traveler and the Fortune", c. 300 B.C.

Fate is determined by what one does and what one doesn't do.
        Ralph Ellison, "Remembering Richard Wright"

YOU AND ME AGAIN

Who would have thought a man whom thought
He was incapable of loving could ever love again
Who would have thought the person close to him
Given the title of a friend
Would be the one he'd love in the end
Who would have ever thought we would see this day
That he'd greet you with a ring in hand
And you'd say those three letters, forming two words
Who would have ever thought
I was meant for you and that you were meant for me
Now let us seal our vows with a kiss
A kiss full of love, joy, and happiness
Who would have ever thought that in the end
It would be you and me again
Our love was brought together by fate
I always knew it would be you and me in the end

CORNELL HURLEY JR.

By the time the fool has learned the game, the players have dispersed.
    Ashanti

The fool is thirsty in the midst of water.
    Ethiopia

So So

Your voice is alluring
So much so
That one could listen all day
Your eyes are captivating
So much so
That one can't possibly look away
Your lips are seductive
So much so
One wishes to kiss you when they can't
Your unfaithful ways
Should cause one to run away
But for your love they'd stay
Because there is just
Oh so much about you
That one just refuses to let slip away
I love you
So much so
I'd endure the pain of loving you
In hope that one day you'd love me the same

CORNELL HURLEY JR.

We believed—because we were young…and had nothing as yet to risk.
	Paule Marshall, "Reena", in Clarke, ed., American Negro Short Stories 1966

To be a great champion you must believe you are the best. If you are not pretend you are.
	Muhammad Ali, speech given at Dacca, Bangladesh

Do You

Do you believe that
What is meant to be will be
Do you believe in love
A feeling that can't be explained
And all that it can be
Do you believe in beliefs
Because if so
Could you see yourself believing in me
I need you to believe
You and I
Are meant to be
These words are not only beliefs but factual
Now do you believe in me

CORNELL HURLEY JR.

It is a hard thing to live haunted by the ghost of an untrue dream.
    W.E.B. Dubois, The Soul of Black Folks, 1903

Hope is delicate suffering.
    Leroi Jones, Home: Social Essay, 1966

Hopes and Dreams

I bargained with life
For my hopes and dreams
The price of faith is all I had to pay
And surely I gained everything

CORNELL HURLEY JR.

It's the plan, not the man.
            Slogan of Congressional Black Caucus, c. 1970

Progress is the attraction that moves humanity.
            Marcus Garvey, Garvey and Garveyism 1963

The Crops

Surely you shall pay what you owe
As a farmer in time reaps what was sown
In time you will without a doubt grow old
What is expected will come to be
When the harvests will come no one knows
We'll just have to wait and see
But surely by now we know that it is destined to be

CORNELL HURLEY JR.

Mama didn't raise no fool.
    Traditional

Silence is all the genius a fool has.
    Zora Neale Hurston, Moses, Man of the Mountain 1939

STUPID LOVE

Stupid is as stupid does
So stupid we are to fall in love
No answer for all of the specifics
So we answer love with all of the above
So if stupid is as stupid does
You must be insane to fall in love
I wasn't stupid but loving you was
Stupid as the situation between you and I was
Somehow we fell deeper in love
Not realizing how stupid it was
If love was meant to heal
Why does it hurt the way it does
I once had a lover try and teach me the ways of love
But she didn't know that love is just as stupid
As the one who falls in love
It is what it is
Stupid is as stupid does
So is love

CORNELL HURLEY JR.

You can take the chains off arms, but not off minds.
    Traditional

Ellis Island is for people who came over on ships. My people came in chains.
    David Dinkins, in Being There Vanity Fair January 1991

Skin of the Sea

The bottom of the sea goes unnoticed
No one walks the floor of the sea
Documenting things that go unnoticed
I can see it clearly from here
With my third eye open at the bottom of the sea
I see plenty lives floating
Bones covered by sand shattered and broken
I see children lost at sea but most of their lives were stolen
Imagine being thrown overboard because of a foreign sickness
Throwing up while unable to control it
Sharks circle nearby
Waiting for black bodies to hit the water
Parting the sea so they can decompose them
In the belly of the ship where most will wait
Being rocked by a mother whose child she hates
Most can't sleep they'll stay awake to see
What the final destination may truly be
The land of opportunity but none for you and me
The land of the brave but on you and I fear is engraved
I'd rather die free resting in peace at the bottom of the sea
Than to enter the land of the slaves

Woman without man is like a field without seed.
    Ethiopia

When you see an arrow that is not going to miss you, throw out your chest and meet it head on.
    Congo

Love Search

Am I to spend all of my days looking for love
I don't even know why I look for love
I've searched here, I've searched there
To be honest with you I've searched everywhere
I've searched high, I've searched low
And still can't find a thing
I even searched around once more
Looking underneath and in between
Love is a good hider because until this very day
I continue to look and still can't find a thing

CORNELL HURLEY JR.

A man has to saddle his dreams before he can ride them.
    Traditional

I am indeed, a practical dreamer. My dreams are not airy nothings. I want to convert my dreams into realities as far as possible.
    Mohandas Gandhi, c. 1940

Just Dream

Dream if you will
Allow your mind to expand
As far as it will
Every obstacle is only a mountain, valley, or hill
There are no limitations simply continue to climb
Accomplish all that was thought of in cotton fields
Thoughts that couldn't become reality
Which can now be put in motion
If only you dared climb the mountains and hills
Cross the valleys in between
At the top of your hills and mountains
You will find that dreams are thoughts of what could be your reality
If only you would find the courage to climb

Nothing can stop you from wishing. You can't beat nobody down so low till you can rob them of their will.
  Ibid

Where there is no vision, the people perish.
  Ibid

SMILE

I wonder what those big lips hide
Truthfully I just wish that you'd smile
I wonder what I'd see if you open wide
I'm in love with your lips but curious about the other side
Be honest with me
What is it that you hide
Is it that you're shy
Or maybe it's a gap-tooth smile
Your teeth may be
Bucked, missing, or buttered but I'd love to see
Because I know it would be worthwhile
At the end of the day when it's all said and done
Truthfully I just wish that you'd smile

CORNELL HURLEY JR.

What matters is not to know the world but to change it.
　　Frantz Fanon, Black Skin, White Mask 1967

He was against all change, except the kind that jingled in his pocket.
　　William Hastie, In Person and Affairs, 28 April 1934

Change

Even the leaves grow old and fall
Summer days go dim bringing forth a chill
Beautiful bundles of joy
Become grey and old
The only thing constant is change
So love me for who I am
But surely that too shall change

CORNELL HURLEY JR.

Let no man of us budge one step, and let slaveholders come to beat us from our country. America is more our country than it is the whites—we have enriched it with our blood and tears. The greatest riches in all America have arisen from our blood and tears.
    David Walker, 1892

The bible ought to teach him that he will become a black angel and go home to a Black God at death.
    Marcus Garvey, 1923

The Word

Down on one knee in a hail Caesar stance
Head bowed at the pews
Praying to the all-forgiving man
White skin, blue eyes, blond hair
Mama said I should praise the man
In the days of slavery he vowed to deliver us
To the Promised Land so is this it
The land of the free, the home of the brave
The land overflowing with the sweat and blood of slaves
People from all over come to visit the USA
Still known to my people
As the home of slaves
Now let us bow our heads and pray

CORNELL HURLEY JR.

The blacker the berry, the sweeter the juice.
    Traditional

Pretty can only get prettier, but beauty compounds itself.
    J. Kennedy Ellington, in Ibid

Blaq Berries

The sweetest juice
Relieves the pain from my aching tooth
Thicker than oil, smooth like satin
My dark juice sends a trickle down my spine
Which delivers thoughts of sexual sensation to my mind
Blaq Berries
Seem to make the sweetest of juice
Quenching my thirst every time
Blaq Berries
Have the sweetest juice of all time
My oh my a mouth full of blaq berries
Calls for a situation where a man must surely take his time

Even though the old man is strong and hearty, he will never live forever.
 Ashanti

Don't gasp at a miracle that is truly miraculous because the magic lies in the fact that you knew it was there for you all along.
 Toni Morrison, Beloved 1987

Ain't Seasonal

My love ain't seasonal
No crumbled leaves beneath my feet
My love ain't just seasonal
Full of rainy days making you weak
My love ain't just seasonal
Winter storms bring forth blistering cold
Causing you to hide away
My love ain't just seasonal
It's full of sunshine and beautiful days
It's full-time this love of mine
It ain't just seasonal

CORNELL HURLEY JR.

All the world fears time, but times fears the pyramids.
    Egypt

Time destroys all things.
    Nigeria

Finite

I couldn't see the love you gave was finite
I imagined the years together we'd spend
But your love didn't survive the first minute
I put my mind, my body, and my soul in it
Only to find out that your heart was overdrawn
With no love remaining in it
However, I'd still give my life
To live in that finite moment
With you in it

CORNELL HURLEY JR.

War begins where reason ends.
    Frederick Douglass, December 1866

The cause of war is preparation for war.
    W.E.B. Du Bois, 1914

Protection

I'm in need of insurance time and time again
Because it ends up broken again
Otter Boxes offer protection but somehow not for this
When bent out of shape an Otter Box won't fix it
Glass would shatter leaving it prone to trouble again
Wood wouldn't last long rotting away allowing viruses in it
I've tried protecting it time and time again
No matter how hard I try
It slips right through the palms of my hands
No matter how hard I try, I always give in
My heart has a mind of its own
Though my mind is troubled, my heart refuses to be alone
So why should I trust you with it
When it's been broken again and again
I'm in desperate need of protection
So that my heart won't reach its limit
Bending out of shape and breaking again

CORNELL HURLEY JR.

The city has conquered me/though it cause me pain/I love its bewitching spell/that's rampant in my brain.
    John Henrick Clarke

Start where you are and move to position of control in your own community.
    Haki Madhubuti, February 1988

Ole MS, Renova

On down the road from Jackson
There's an old town
That nobody knows
Full of trailer homes
And gravel roads
On down the road from Jackson
There's an old town that nobody knows
Full of hearts made of gold
Empty warehouse rusted and old
Leaving many unemployed and alone
On down the road from Jackson
There's an old town
Where I no longer go
A place I once roamed
Along gravel roads
On down memory lane
A place I no longer know
On down the road from Jackson
A little old town I once called home

CORNELL HURLEY JR.

THE CONCRETE JUNGLE BEARS NO SHADE

CORNELL HURLEY JR.

Respect me or put me to death.
    Malcolm X, 1964

The respect that is only bought with gold is not worth much. It is no honor to shake hands politically with men who whip and steal babies.
    Frances E.W. Harper, 1859

Respect

See you may ask for it
Me on the other hand
I demand it
It's never handed out
Nor is it paid for
It has to be earned or at times demanded
As a man
I refuse to do without it
While some may shout, pout, and cry about it
I'm ready and always willing
To stand up and die about it

CORNELL HURLEY JR.

The hot winds of change, blowing through the central city ghettos...are producing an articulate group of young people who possess the seed of hope for tomorrow.
    Samuel B McKinney, 1972

The wind and the water had given life to lots of things that folks think of as dead and given death to so much that had been living.
    Zora Neale Hurston, 1937

SEASONS

Seasons are in constant change
You came in my life around September
Oh how I miss you
My sweet summer rain
I'd fallen to my knees
As leaves tend to do when the weather changes
In the winter you came
Bringing forth a blistering pain
Placing an icebox around my heart
Leaving freezing cold blood running through my veins
In fall you changed my view on things
You showed me life wasn't always green
The lessons I learned from you will always remain
Though you were only a fling
I didn't expect for you to change
I guess what we shared
Was only a seasonal thing

CORNELL HURLEY JR.

Growth always involves the risk of failure.
    Howard Thurman, 1963

The greatest failure for any man is to fail with a woman.
    Chester Himes, 1972

Loss of a Loser

I hate to lose something
He sadly bowed his head
Especially my time
I'd rather die instead
I can't explain it, what more can I say
Just know that I hate to lose something
I once lost my action figure
I must have cried for days
He had a kung-fu grip with a military fade
Someone must have taken him away
More than likely a thief
Just know that I hate to lose something
My car crunk up and drove away
It was covered in candy paint
That would shine no matter the time of day
Never will I forget it
And even after all that
Just know that I hate to lose something
A loser I am, I've lost a lot
Some may say all, but I would say not
Because I still have my boo the sweetest joy of 'em all
Though I continue to lose she keeps me standing tall

CORNELL HURLEY JR.

It's much easier to show compassion to animals. They are never wicked.
    Haile Selassie, c. 1940

You can't base your life on other people's expectations.
    Stevie Wonder, c. 1988

Difference Is

I must have done a good job
Loving you because it seem impossible
For you to love me the way I loved you
For you I swear my love was true
But you just couldn't love me the way I loved you
That was the only difference between us two
You couldn't love me the way that I loved you

CORNELL HURLEY JR.

I no longer need the past to stand up in the present.
    Edouard Maunick, 1964

I freed thousands of slaves, I could have freed thousands more, if they had known they were slaves.
    Harriet Tubman, c. 1865

Flashback

I recall days darker than my flesh
Though I was yet to be born
Even with history being told foul
I've sought and somehow I've found
I can feel the whip and the breeze that it brings
Drops of sweat and the awful sting
I'd run but where would I go
Chased down by bloodhounds
Only to be captured and drowned in memories
Of what used to be
Flashbacks of a land far away
Flashbacks of a time I was once free
Now incarcerated by history and thoughts of what used to be
Flashbacks of those who died for me

CORNELL HURLEY JR.

He who receives a gift doesn't measure.
    Ivory Coast

One does not give a gift without motive.
    Mali

A Gift

The present is a present within itself
To be in the moment in which we shared
Was nothing more than a gift
That I am proud to have shared with you
A gift within a box
Are the ones where you and I remain the same
A 4x6 without a frame
We had all that we ever wanted
What a beautiful gift it was
A gift given then taken away
Your love was mine to keep with no receipt
I wouldn't dare give it back
Your love grew on me
So today I'm asking you
To give my love back because gifts are given
With the intentions of lasting forever
Even though you and I knew that our love wouldn't last forever

Always listen. Be careful when you speak because the bush has ears.
    Guyana

Add a third to your ears even if it be an imaginary one, for the news is so enchanting that two ears are not enough.
    Hausa

Don't Hold Your Breath

Hold your breath
If only for a moment
Listen for just a second
Then maybe you'll hear the story
My heart tells when lonely
A long story indeed
But it will only take a moment
In order for you to notice
My heart is sincere and honest
And the story it tells
Is all about how you
Left it brokenhearted and lonely
Would I be wrong
To wish that you'd stay around
Patiently holding your breath forever
Listening to my heart's every word as it extends the story
Hoping that you may hold your breath for a while longer
Listen to my heart
If only for a moment

Let your love be like the misty rains, coming softly, but flooding the river.
    Madagascar

The less one loves a woman, the surer one is of possessing her.
    Ibid

This Weekend

I thought about you this weekend
I wondered if you were thinking too
I thought about you this weekend
I thought about you for so long
I think I thought of just about
All of the things we could possibly do
I thought about you this weekend
Truth be told I thought about all that we could do
If only your occupation would unshackle you
And allow for you to be free
There would be no limits
To what we could be
I thought about you this weekend
Every night until I'd fall asleep
In those moments my thoughts turned into beautiful dreams
I could feel you here next to me
I thought about you this weekend
Hopefully you thought of me too
During the week I feel close to you
And on weekends I'm lonely without you
I thought about you this weekend
Wondered if you were thinking too
Because I have nothing planned for the weekend
Other than thinking of you
My love this weekend, I can only hope
That you think of me too

CORNELL HURLEY JR.

The blues is where we come from and what we experience. The blues came from nothingness, from want and desire.
    W.C. Handy, c. 1918

But softly/as the tunes come from his throat/trouble/mellows to a golden note.
    Langston Hughes, 1959

You're Mine

Though you have my heart and soul
There were many before you
So excuse me when I say
It's hard to believe
You won't just up and leave
Your bars hold me captive
Your lyrics give me sight
Your words cause my deepest emotions to surface
And though your rhythm makes me groove
It's still hard to believe
You won't just up and leave
This is for you
My first love
Always and forever
Rhythm and blues

CORNELL HURLEY JR.

Where there is no future, there is no hope.
    Edward Wilmot Blyden, 1865

Some unknown natural phenomenon occurs which cannot be explained and a new local demigod is named.
    Zora Neale Hurston, 1925

Small Town Girl

I wrote this with tears in my eyes
But with too much pride to let one show
My interest in you has become an array of emotions
Which I can no longer control
My interest in you was once physical
Looking deep into your brown eyes
I read a story so deep and full of pain
I wouldn't walk one mile in your shoes
With one of mines even if I had nine lives
Don't get me wrong from you I wouldn't run
Your story I'm intrigued by
A small town girl that captured her dreams
It takes commitment to do such a thing
So commit to me and I'll commit to you
You offer a love
That I wouldn't trade for the world
A love that I would not only live but die for
So I will always remember the small town girl
That chased her dreams and passed me by

CORNELL HURLEY JR.

If the blues was whiskey, I'd stay drunk all the time, stay drunk, baby just to wear you off my mind.
    Blues

It's all in the mind. You can get just as high if you did deep breathing.
    Sidney Bechet, c. 1946

True Love

I live for love
I would even die for love
Drop down and pray for love
Many say that they love me
Ironic as it may seem I can't feel the love
Give me death
Or give me love
Because I can't go without it
Love is what I crave
An addict I am for love
Love is extremely potent
The world's most famous drug
Indescribable the things I'd do for love
True love that is
I crave like a drug
I don't know what I wouldn't do for true love

CORNELL HURLEY JR.

There was nothing more to lose. Being that far down he was no longer afraid to fall.
    Charles Johnson, 1990

Stretch our mind and fly.
    Traditional

I Won't Fall

I keep on falling but today I stand
I continue to fall when my legs give way
Though I fall again I rise
At night I fall closing my eyes
Then again in the morning I rise
There is nothing or no one
Who could possibly hold me down
They love when I am crippled and beaten down
For in the moment I cannot rise
My legs are on strike, they refuse move
But no matter what happens it'll soon end
Running, jumping, and kicking again
I will rise and rise again
Until my final day I will soar
To a height that has no end
I will rise but not to stand
Because this time I will fly
Never to descend again

CORNELL HURLEY JR.

If I'm all you have, then I'm all you need.
    Traditional

Who is the more in fault in an erring passion, she who falls through entreaty, or he who entreats her to fall?
    Juana De La Cruz, 1670

Reflect

The sky is only a reflection
A reelection of the waters below
The waters below are only a reflection
Of the heavens above
The reflection in your eyes
When I stand before you
Shows an image of your true love
So what is it you see when you stand before me
If my heart is a reflection of your heart
Then you should see just as I do
It's clear the reflection in our eyes
Should show that our love is true

CORNELL HURLEY JR.

Proverbs are the daughters of experience.
    Sierra Leone

She is proverb of propriety.
    Alexandre Dumas, 1855

Past Love

Pushed aside swept under the rug
No longer thought about
Forgotten amongst a list of other words
Describes my thoughts of what was
Underneath the sole of your shoe
Is where my heart lies as you run away
From what was once love
I'm soon to be a crushed love bug

CORNELL HURLEY JR.

People strive to lose themselves among other people. This they do because of their lack of knowledge of self.
    Elijah Muhammad, 1962

Trust yourself. Think of yourself. Act for yourself. Speak for yourself. Be yourself. Imitation is suicide.
    Marva Collins, c. 1988

ME MYSELF AND I

Me myself and I
At times I don't know who I am
I've been living a lie
Me myself and I
Me personally, I find it hard to believe
How is it that I don't understand I
Me myself and I
Myself it's my fault
Of course I'm to blame
I've been paying so much attention
To everyone else lately
I forgot about who
Me, myself, and even I was

CORNELL HURLEY JR.

THE CONCRETE JUNGLE BEARS NO SHADE

CORNELL HURLEY JR.

Where there is no experience of pain, there can be no suffering.
    Howard Thurman, 1963

It's the little hurts that build up.
    Ishmael Reed, 1988

JUST MAINTAIN

Sitting in silence with a hallowed brain
Red dots nor a steady hand would change a thing
Shallow distance point blank range
Surrounded by complete darkness
Should I release the spark of the barrel
In hope that I may see the light
Or in complete darkness should I remain
My friends all sound cliché
All saying the same old thang
Everything's going to be just fine
You just have to maintain
As if they've felt the same pain
Russian roulette without a revolver
Is definitely an unfair game
But I like the odds
Because quite frankly I'm sick and tired of all the pain
My boy told me the other day
He tried offing himself
Instead of asking why or offering help
I paid close attention listening for suggestions
While thinking of offing myself
Then he hit me with that cliché shit
It'll be alright, I promise
You just got to maintain
Knowing that he and I never felt the same pain
Now here I am once again
Thinking about putting one in my brain
I guess him and I must have felt the same pain
Now in my hallowed brain
There is only one thing that remains
A lonely echo that constantly rings

CORNELL HURLEY JR.

Saying you just got to maintain
I wonder if he thought the same thing
Before pulling the trigger and putting one in his brain

THE CONCRETE JUNGLE BEARS NO SHADE

CORNELL HURLEY JR.

What is said of the dead lion's body could not be said to him alive.
    Congo

I am not going to die, I'm going home like a shooting star.
    Sojourner Truth, 1883

The Last Time

If I'd known it was the last time
I would have spoken more sincere for the last time
I would have spoken of memories we shared
Or at least the memory of our last time together
At least one last time
If only I'd known it was the last time
Though I had no idea that it was going to be our last time
I'm excited I spoke those three words
One last time
So through these words I pray
That you feel the gratitude of my love
One last time

CORNELL HURLEY JR.

How good for a son to grasp his father's words. He will reach old age through them.
    Ptah Hotep, c. 2340 B.C.

I feel privileged to be his son. I am happy to have had him, if only for a little while.
    Julius Garvey, 1986

My Boy

Thinking of all the things
You and I couldn't do
I shed tears of diamonds for you
No ABCs or counting to three
I really wanted to be there
To teach you those things
To see that first breath
Or you taking that first step
If I could turn back the hands of time
I would be there with you
Like a father should at the drop of a dime
If I only had one wish
I would wish that you'd stay young
So that one day I could carry you in my arms
As you grow older and life begins to change
Know that you will always be my boy
That's one thing for certain that won't change

CORNELL HURLEY JR.

THE CONCRETE JUNGLE BEARS NO SHADE

CORNELL HURLEY JR.

THE CONCRETE JUNGLE BEARS NO SHADE

CORNELL HURLEY JR.

I can see farther over the mountain than the man who is standing atop of it.
    Gulla

It's hard for young players to see the big picture. They just see three or four years down the road.
    Kareem Abdul-Jabbar, 1986

Mental Photographs

I close my eyes flipping through the pages
Yet still afraid of what I may find
Like a love I thought would last a lifetime
Reminds me over time love and life change
Love however will survive the fight
And without you I'm still alright
With the images now in my mind
Proves I would have given my life for you a million times

CORNELL HURLEY JR.

I have no need to cross my fingers while speaking to you. It's as if you see right through me, so I open my heart easily when talking to you. Without my fingers crossed I would like to say I love you and hopefully one day we both can say I do.
    Cornell Hurley Jr.

Fingers Crossed

I swear to tell the truth
Every word I've written was true
Fingers crossed
If I were to lose you
I have no idea as in what I might do
Fingers crossed
With my hands out of sight
I say that I love you
From the bottom of my heart
My lover, my woman, my best friend
Fingers crossed
I try not to laugh
Because without my fingers crossed
I wouldn't have spoken the half
Fingers crossed
I know it's a childish thing
But you and I both know
That love is dangerous but yet a childish game

CORNELL HURLEY JR.

THE CONCRETE JUNGLE BEARS NO SHADE

CORNELL HURLEY JR.

A prison has a door, but a grave hasn't.
    Alexandre Dumas, 1844

Behind bars a man never reforms. He will never forget. He will never completely get over the memories of the bars.
    Malcolm X, 1965

How It Feels

How will it feel to be
Finally on the other side where I dream to be
I wonder how it will feel to see
The simple wonders of the world
Because for years they were things I couldn't see
How will it feel to explore the world
Traveling to places I never thought I'd be
I wonder how it will feel
To finally one day be free

CORNELL HURLEY JR.

LOVE

If I had to choose one word to describe who I am, that word would be none other than love. My philosophy on life is quite simple, love conquers all. Without love nothing would exist, think about that for a moment. Imagine there was no you nor me, not even this book which you hold within your hands would exist. Simply put love is the process in which all creations are brought to life. For the Higher Power created and gave us life, which is why we shall never fall from grace, not because we're perfect but because of the love the Higher Power has for us. However, you should know that love has no clear definition unless it's contained within a dictionary. Love can be described in an innumerable amount of ways and displayed in countless ways.

I still recall the day I was escorted out of my home by Montgomery County Police. That's the day I decided that I was going to rid my heart of love. For the crime in which I was accused of committing I knew that I was going away for a while. Though I'd never been incarcerated for a great period of time before, I knew exactly what to expect. From what I'd learned from the streets, I knew a man in prison had no room for love in his heart or so I thought. I made it a point from the moment those cuffs were put on my wrists I was going to be exactly who they thought I was in order to survive.

Being the guy who people thought I was based on the crime that I had committed allowed for me to pretend as if everything was fine. I was pretending as if I wasn't mad that my freedom had been taken away. I pretended as if I had no part in anything that had gone wrong. I wasn't the one to blame, it was everyone around me who was fucked up, not me. Truth be told being angry allowed me to blame everyone but myself. Honestly, I was afraid of what was to come, I was scared of the life sentence I was facing, scared because of the nightmares that kept me up at night, and I was afraid to lose everything that I'd worked for.

For a while I didn't call anyone back home, the sound of a familiar voice was too much for me to handle. It's true what they say, when you get locked up anyone who truly cares for you is locked up too. I could hear the pain in the voices of the ones who loved me but I refused to acknowledge the hurt. I could not feel sorry for them nor myself if I were to survive in the concrete jungle. No matter how far I ran, no matter where I hid, love always seemed to find me. I was getting more love than I ever had before on the outside. From family members, to friends, even a few staff members were showing love. The more love they showed the less angry I became. It was in that time when I felt love that I realized what I'd been missing out on all along, love. Without the love everyone showed me I wouldn't have written this book. It's like I stated before, love truly does conquer all. Receiving and giving love is a beautiful thing, you just have to be man or woman enough to open up your heart after feeling the pain.

About the Author

Cornell Hurley Jr.'s story is a stride towards a second chance. He is a loving husband, a father, and a brother that has always been willing to give his all to help anyone. A few years ago, there was a tragedy that caused a major shift and separation from his unborn child, who was only a month away at the time of his incarceration, his wife, and his family members. Things were starting to get better for him and his family. Cornell was looking forward to being a father and was on the verge of becoming a NCO within the United States Army. His dreams and desires were put on hold and shattered in the year of 2015 after an unexpected incident took place.

In February 2015, Cornell went out for a night of celebration with other close military friends. A fight happened while amongst others in the crowd on the dance floor of a local nightclub. Shortly after, a certain individual started it back up and would not allow the situation to calm down. There were accusations towards him and a lot of instigation going back and forth of misleading information. Cornell was thrown out of the local nightclub with the same crowd of individuals who had assaulted him in the nightclub. There was factual evidence proving that Cornell did not start this incident which would end tragically.

As he was preparing to leave, he was cornered and surrounded by a group of five males, some of which had already assaulted him inside of the nightclub. There was no one to come to his rescue to defuse the situation which had gotten completely out of hand. He was separated from his friends with no security guards anywhere to shine light in a dark and difficult situation as he would end up fighting for his life.

The other party was parked across the street from the establishment where the incident occurred but continued to follow Cornell as he ran to his car which was parked behind the building. Imagine being chased down and outnumbered by a group of guys whom have minutes before just assaulted you, with no friends around and not knowing if anyone had a weapon on them. It was stated during the court hearing that the victims could be heart shouting, "Let's go get him." After the attackers closed in on Cornell, he fired several warning shots hoping to cause his attackers to back off but was unsuccessful. During the firing of several warning shots, someone was killed.

Evidence and facts from the court proceedings show that Cornell did not start the fight and was not the aggressor at any point during the tragic event. Even with all of the evidence presented before the court Cornell was sentenced to 25 years at the age of 25. The media made Cornell Hurley Jr. to look as though he was a monster which society should rid itself of. However, what you should know about the author of this book is that he should not be defined by the charges in which he was found guilty of but the content of his heart. Forgiveness was granted to Cornell on the day of his sentencing by the family members of the deceased victim from that deadly night. This meant the world to him, even though he was going to have his freedom taken away and he was not going to be in his son's life for an unknown amount of years, he felt a burden had been lifted off his shoulders.

Like all stories there is a beginning, middle, and an end. The story of the author is still being written as you read these words. Cornell is quickly approaching his first parole date and looking forward to being released so that he can finally rewrite his wrongs.

KaNeisha Thomas

Cornell Hurley
1300 N. Warehouse Road
United States Disciplinary Barracks
Fort Leavenworth, Kansas 66027
19 April 2021

After the war is over there are still battles to be won. There are battles in which service members and veterans must desperately fight. Service members and veterans at the United States Disciplinary Barracks have been fighting a battle that we cannot win. We are in need of outside influence so that our voices may be heard and our stories may be told. Will you help us fight the unlawful actions in which we're subject to daily while in military confinement?

To be a law-abiding citizen is all that most people deem necessary in order to be an American citizen. However, being a law-abiding citizen is not enough for the elite. There is no law requiring men and women to go above and beyond for their country. Pledging allegiance to the flag and being patriotic is just not enough. Desperately searching for methods in which one may further honor their country in all matters foreign and domestic. The elite citizens become Soldiers, Sailors, Airmen, and Marines for their country, which is no easy task, for great sacrifices must be made. These service members all fight to ensure that the laws of the land are abided by foreign and domestic alike. Equality and justice for all is what our service members fight and die for. Sacrificing their time with their families and even sacrificing their own lives for something in which they will never partake in thousands of service members are incarcerated in military facilities here in America, over-sentenced and unlawfully convicted. The Uniform Code of Military Justice (UCMJ) is flawed and needs to be exposed and corrected immediately. The military confining facilities are practicing unlawful practices from within as well that needs to be exposed. The military law is completely different from the laws in which those incarcerated service members vowed to fight and die for.

CNN, Fox News, MSNBC, and many other media outlets have brought attention to war crimes. The media gave service members who have been accused of committing crimes on foreign land a second chance at life by making sure their voices were heard. While the battle cries of the remaining incarcerated service members who have been accused of committing domestic offenses are unlawfully convicted and treated as if they are enemies of the United States of America. Everyday citizens are entitled to a fair trial, and they receive just that. While the same service members who fought to defend the liberties of this great country fall victim to military justice through courts-martial. Despite losing their freedom, liberty, rank, and the right to ever wear their uniforms again, service members are not asking for favors, but for the same justice to be afforded to them which they have earned, but we should be granted a second chance to be treated as everyday citizens in a court of law and not be subjected to heavily flawed, unfair, and biased Uniform Code of Military Justice.

If you are willing to help, I ask that you please respond. If you are not able to help, I ask that you please guide us in the direction of someone who might be able or willing to provide help. Thank you for your time and consideration with this matter.

Cornell Hurley
Veteran, U.S. Army

CORNELL HURLEY JR.

Appendix

November 9, 2020

As a child I write this entry. I am no longer afraid of what may lay ahead of me. Today is the day I begin to embrace life with all of its flaws. My smile is genuine and the love which I give is pure. My imagination is strong, there are no limits as in what I can do. Starting today I set out on a journey to become a new man.

I am,
Cornell Hurley

THE CONCRETE JUNGLE BEARS NO SHADE

November 9, 2020

As a child I write this entry. I am no longer afraid of what may lay ahead of me. Today is the day I begin to embrace life with all of it's flaws. My smile is genuine and the love which I give is pure. My imagination is strong, there are no limits as in what I can do. Starting today I set out on a journey to become a new man.

I am,

November 10, 2020

The white man never has separated Christianity from white, nor has he separated the white man from Christianity. When you hear a white man bragging, "I'm a Christian," he's bragging about being a white man. Then you have the Negro. – Malcolm X

The Word
Down on bending knees
Hail Caesar stance
Head bowed at the pews
Praying to the all-forgiving man
White skin, blue eyes, blond hair
Mama said to praise the man
In days of slavery
He vowed to deliver us
To the promised land
So this is it
The land of the free
Home of the brave
Overflowing with sweat and blood
Of slaves

The U.S.A.
Home of the KKK
Still known to me and mine
As the home of slaves
No longer will we
Pray for a better day
It's time to fight
Fist balled up tight
In unison
Is the only way
For us to make
A better way
Now let us pray

THE CONCRETE JUNGLE BEARS NO SHADE

November 10, 2020

"The white man never has seperated Christianity from white, nor has he seperated the white man from Christianity. When you hear a white man bragging, "I'm a Christian," he's bragging about being a white man. Then you have the Negro." — Malcom X —

The Word

Down on bending knees
hail Ceasar stance
head bowed at the pews
praying to the all forgiving man
  White skin, blue eyes, blond hair
  mama said to praise the man
In days of slavery
he vowed to deliver us
to the promise land
  So this is it
  the land of the free
  home of the brave
overflowing with sweat and blood
of slaves

The U.S.A
home of the KKK
Still known to me & mine
as the home of slaves
No longer will we
pray for a better day
its time to fight
fist balled up tight
in unison
is the only way
for us to make
a better way
Now let us pray

November 18, 2020

Though my view of the horizon is tainted from my cell window, I admire it daily. My view, infected by massive gray bricks and barbed wire, which the sun adorns is still a lovely sight to see. Watching the sun run beyond the horizon, I rise to my feet wishing I could closely follow. With faith that I may watch her rise in the morning, I muster the pain inside. For Allah, the creator all things, is the master artist. Tomorrow's sky surely will not be the same as it was today but I will continue looking beyond my window for better days. Allah the master artist will not duplicate the sky from the day prior. So whether sunrise or sunset I will constantly be looking for you.

Illusions,

Cornell Hurley

THE CONCRETE JUNGLE BEARS NO SHADE

November 18, 2020

Though my view of the horizon is tainted from my cell window, I admire it daily. My view, infected by massive grey bricks and barbwire, which the sun adorns is still a lovely sight to see. Watching the sun run beyond the horizon, I rise to my feet wishing I could closely follow. With faith that I may watch her rise in the morning, I master the pain inside. For Allah, the creator of all things is the master artist. Tomorrow's sky surely will not be the same as it was today but I will continue looking beyond my window for better days. Allah the master artist will not duplicate the sky from the day prior. So whether sunrise or sunset I will constantly be looking for you.

Illusions,

November 21, 2020

Being incarcerated has caused me to forget that the world is in constant motion. People are moving from place to place while I sit stagnate with many years ahead of me. As a child my mother would constantly have to remind me that I had no need to be in a hurry. Like most adolescents I chased daylight as if it were not to return. I question whether my mother would say the same today? All the people I've given my heart to and life itself has seemed to have passed me by. However, once I'm done serving this time I will be just fine. I must constantly remind myself that I have no need to rush things. I'll be just fine.

Time,
Cornell Hurley

THE CONCRETE JUNGLE BEARS NO SHADE

November 21, 2020

Being incarcerated has caused me to forget that the world is in constant motion. People are moving from place to place, while I sit stagnate with many years ahead of me. As a child my mother would constantly have to remind me that I had no need to be in a hurry. Like most adolescents I chased daylight as if it were not to return. I question whether my mother would say the same today? All the people I've given my heart to and life itself has seemed to have passed me by. However, once I'm done serving this time I will be just fine. I must constantly remind myself that I have no need to rush things. I'll be just fine.

Time

30 November 2020

My heart is stubborn and wants what it wants regardless of what my mind may think. I need you unlike I have ever needed you before. Like an infant needs its mother I need you. Confusing as it may seem I do not need you but I want you badly. Long ago I chose you and in doing so I made the decision to stay with you for better or worse. Without a piece of paper and without a ring I made you my wife. We set our own standard as in how we'd love one another. So where are you now that I need you? Truth is at the moment neither of us truly know what we want. You're afraid of the time in which I serve which will surely end. I understand. If you come back again our love will never be the same. You nor the love you give can ever be trusted again.

THE CONCRETE JUNGLE BEARS NO SHADE

30 November 2020

My heart is stubborn and wants what it wants regaurdless of what my mind may think. I need you unlike I have ever needed you before. Like an infant needs its mother I need you. Confusing as it may seem I do not need you but I want you badly. Long ago I chose you and in doing so I made the decision to stay with you for better or worse. Without a piece of paper and without a ring I made you my wife. We set our own standard as in how we'd love one another. So where are you now that I need you? Truth is at the moment neither of us truly know what we want. You're afraid of the time in which I serve which will surely end. I understand. If you come back again our love will never be the same. You nor the love you give can ever be trusted again.

$\frac{11}{38}$ WTF!

December 7, 2020

I was once close to having the love that I always dreamed of. I was a spoken word away, a simple step away, and a heartbeat away from what I still search for today. I allowed doubt to conquer my mind. I gave up. I was somewhat defeated by love. I was afraid of what I didn't know about love, so I let it go. I vow the next time I feel a burning desire within my heart, I won't give up.

Main goal,
Cornell Hurley

THE CONCRETE JUNGLE BEARS NO SHADE

Dec 7, 2020

I was once close to having the love that I always dreamed of. I was a spoken word away, a simple step away, and a heartbeat away from what I still search for today. I allowed doubt to conquer my mind. I gave up. I was somewhat defeated by love. I was afraid of what I didn't know about ♥ so I let it go. I vow the next time I feel a burning desire within my heart, I won't give up.

CORNELL HURLEY JR.

December 15, 2020

To just bow down and accept defeat, who the fuck would I be? I don't exactly know who I'd be, but I do fear that bowing down would make me less than a black man. Every morning I rise from my bed until the next time I do so again. I will always and 4ever remain a black man. So know that it isn't part of my nature to bow before cowards. Behind bars and yet somehow I remain free. Shoot us down for being any complexion of brown and still I refuse to bow. I fear no weapon that may be used by the coward. Being that I am far from a coward, I am ready to die about it. Whatever it may take to live free as a black man.

Black man,
Cornell Hurley

THE CONCRETE JUNGLE BEARS NO SHADE

Dec 15, 2020

To just bow down and accept defeat, who the fuck would I be? I don't exactly know who I'd be but I do fear that bowing down would make me less than a black man. Every morning I rise from my bed until the next time I do so again, I will always & 4ever remain a black man. So know that it isn't part of my nature to bow before cowards. Behind bars and yet somehow I remain free. Shoot us down for being any complexion of brown and still I refuse to bow. I fear no weapon that may be used by the coward. Being that I am far from a coward, I am ready to die about it. Whatever it may take to live free as a black man.

Black man

December 31, 2020

No longer will I hinder myself from the many blessings that await me. Today I am making a decision to stay out of my own way. Wondering what if is now a thing of the past. Starting today I vow to accomplish all goals and to also see that my dreams come to life. Failure is inevitable, however, success is always obtainable. Fuck it. I have no choice but to go all in. Failure is no longer an option.

Dissatisfaction with possession
And achievement is one of the
Requisites to further achievement.
    John Hope

THE CONCRETE JUNGLE BEARS NO SHADE

December 31, 2020

No longer will I hinder myself from the many blessings that await me. Today I am making a decision to 'stay out of my own way.' Wondering what if, is now a thing of the past. Starting today I vow to accomplish all goals and to also see that my dreams come to life. Failure is inevitable, however, success is always obtainable. Fuck it I have no choice but to go all in, failure is no longer a option.

> Dissatisfaction with possession and achievement is one of the requisites to further achievement.
> — John Hope —

January 1, 2021

For so long I blamed you all. The way you made me feel when you said that I was dumb. The way you showed and told me that I would never be good enough. You broke me down to the lowest level and for that I thank you all. You allowed me to fail multiple times. Back then I could not see the beauty within every failure. Now because of you I continue to seek knowledge. I know now that I am way too much for you, and it's because of you that I now welcome failure with open arms. I pray with all my heart that failure soon finds you. I really do. Truth be told I wish that you'd fail in hopes that failure may create a better you. Failure is the key.

Success,
Cornell Hurley

THE CONCRETE JUNGLE BEARS NO SHADE

January 1, 2021

For so long I blamed you all the way you made me feel when you said that I was dumb. The way you screamed and told me that I would never be good enough. You broke me down to the lowest level and for that I thank you all. You allowed me to fail multiple times, back then I could not see the beauty within every failure. Now because of you I continue to seek knowledge. I know now that I am way too much for you, and it's because of you that I now welcome failure with open arms. I pray with all my heart that failure soon finds you, I really do. Truth be told I wish that you'd feel in hopes that failure may create a better you. Failure is the key

Success,

7 January 21

Look at you taking the time out of your day to read my shit. What is it you gain from reading my shit? Would you like to know the real me? Is that why you decide to thumb through my shit? I could care less, go right ahead and continue reading. I don't even know who the fuck I am, so good luck. I heard someone say the only time people are comfortable with accepting death is when they've figured out their purpose in life and once they've reached complete knowledge of self. I don't know if I will ever be willing to accept death but surely without warning one day my death will come.

Stronger I am,
38

THE CONCRETE JUNGLE BEARS NO SHADE

7 January 21

Look at you taking the time out of your day to read my shit. What is it you gain from reading my shit? Would you like to know the real me? Is that why you decide to thumb through my shit? I could care less go right ahead and continue reading. I don't even know who the fuck I am, so good luck. I heard someone say, "The only time people are comfortable with accepting death is when they've figured out their purpose in life and once they've reached complete knowledge of self." I don't know if I will ever be willing to accept death but surely without warning one day my death will come.

Stranger I am,
38

9 January 2021

Sometimes I look at you and I feel as if it's the first time. At times I look at you and I hate what I see. Then there are times when I stare deep into your eyes, looking at the flaws you hide. See they may not see you like I do, but just know that I know the real you. I know you, I know us. Of course I know me.

Mirror,
Cornell Hurley

THE CONCRETE JUNGLE BEARS NO SHADE

9 January 2021

Sometimes I look at you and I feel as if it's the first time. At times I look at you and I hate what I see. Then there are times when I stare deep into your eyes, looking at the flaws you hide. See they may not see you like I do, but just know that I know the real you. I know you, I know us, of course I know me.

Mirror,

17 January 21

This generation had no Douglass, no Powell, no King, no Malcolm to break things down for them.

    Susan Taylor

I've led beautiful women down a path of destruction. Many who considered me to be a lover or friend never knew their worth. Leading them far away from their dreams I was in control. Continuous bouts of sex left their bodies in a complete state of ecstasy, allowing me to control their minds. I enjoyed this false sense of power I had over these females. As a man I must say that because of my actions I've failed. However, I have leadership skills now. My mission now is to lead that special woman to joy, love, and happiness. Who are you? Where are you? God, please lead her to me.

    Leadership

THE CONCRETE JUNGLE BEARS NO SHADE

17 January 21

This generation had no Douglass, no Powell, no King, no Malcom to break things down for them.
— Susan Taylor —

    I've lead beautiful women down a path of destruction. Many who considered me to be a lover or friend, never knew their worth. Leading them far away from their dreams I was in control. Continuous bouts of sex left their bodies in a complete state of ecstasy, allowing me to control their minds. I enjoyed this false sense of power I had over these females. As a man I must say that because of my actions I've failed. However, I have leadership skills now. My mission now is to lead that special woman to joy, love, and happiness. Who are you? Where are you? God please lead her to me.

Leadership

23 January 21

My heart bleeds for the many hearts that I've broken. I knew wrong from right. I was just afraid to follow my heart. Not loving myself allowed for me to love all that you all did for and to me but it also allowed for me to easily hurt you. I never stopped for a second to wonder what type of damage I may have caused. Until now I had no idea how to respect a woman, love a woman, nor did I know how to take care of her needs. Today I know your pain. I now know what it is to give love and not get it back. Today my heart aches. I'm empty inside.

Karma

THE CONCRETE JUNGLE BEARS NO SHADE

23 January 21

My heart bleeds for the many hearts that I've broken. I knew wrong from right, I was just afraid to follow my heart. Not loving myself allowed for me to love all that you all did for and to me but it also allowed for me to easily hurt you. I never stopped for a second to wonder what type of damage I may have caused. Until now I had no idea how to respect a **Woman**, love a woman, nor did I know how to take care of her needs. Today I know your pain. I now know what it is to give love and not get it back. Today my heart aches, I'm empty inside.

Karma,

27 Jan 21

I'm losing my fucking mind thinking about you. I can't help but wonder what I could have possibly done this time around. Shit, I changed for the better in hopes that you'd appreciate me a little more. Shit, I even got out of my comfort zone for you and you alone. I had no room for love in my heart and look at what you did.

I was so proud when you found your way back to me, I almost couldn't believe it. Never have I felt love the way you make me feel loved. I don't think anyone on this earth will ever make me feel as you do.

When it's good between you and I, the world adores what we have. Then when it's bad, it's as if we never knew one another, let alone loved each other. Then like always you leave me alone to wonder where you are. When are you going to grow up and learn how to handle issues like an adult? You can only run away for so long before the truth stands before you. I can only wait for so long before without my heart begins to mend. It's been too long anyway. Fuck love! Fuck you!

THE CONCRETE JUNGLE BEARS NO SHADE

27 Jan 21

I'm losing my fucking mind thinking about you. I can't help but wonder what I could have possibly done this time around. Shit, I changed for the better in hopes that you'd appreciate me a little more. Shit, I even got out of my comfort zone for you and you alone. I had no room for love in my heart and look at what you did.

I was so pissed when you found your way back to me, I almost couldn't believe it. Never have I felt love, the way you make me feel loved. I don't think anyone on this earth will ever make me feel as you do.

When it's good between you and I, the world adores what we have. Then when it's bad, it's as if we never knew one another, yet alone loved each other. Then like always you leave me alone to wonder where you are. When are you going to grow up and learn how to handle issues like an adult. You can only run away for so long before the truth stands before you. I can only wait for so long, before without my heart begins to mend. It's been too long anyway. Fuck Love! Fuck You! ♥

6 Feb 21

Dearly I wish that I was a tree, completely submitted to the will of God. A tree with deeply planted roots that reached beyond the core of the earth. I would most likely be an oak tree, all would admire my strength. The strongest winds would not cause me to budge. For all of those around me I would provide shelter and care. Truly I would have no worries because all of my needs would be provided for. Rain from the sky above and the soil beneath my feet would feed me. There would be many birds and bees to carry my seed, so a legacy I could leave. However, as a human I am tempted daily. I desire to have what is unobtainable. I want LOVE but it's as if love is not for me.

Peace,

38

THE CONCRETE JUNGLE BEARS NO SHADE

6 Feb 21

Dearly, I wish that I was a tree, completely submitted to the will of God. A tree with deeply planted roots that reached beyond the core of the earth. I would most likely be an Oak tree, all would admire my strength. The strongest winds would not cause me to budge. For all of those around me I would provide shelter and care. Truly I would have no worries because all of my needs would be provided for. From the sky above and the soil beneath my feet would feed me. There would be many birds and bees to carry my seed, so a legacy I would leave.

    However, as a human I am tempted daily. I desire to have what is unobtainable. I want **LOVE** but it's as if love is not for me.

                      Peace,
                      38

CORNELL HURLEY JR.

13 Feb 21

Since I can recall I've been searching. I've been on a mission seeking to discover something. I desperately want to discover who I am, what I'm meant to be, and to know if I will be one of the greats. Today I write from a prison cell, not allowing where I am to hinder me. Incarcerated but yet free in my mind, my attitude today is fuck it! Fuck you too, fuck anyone who may have doubted me. Fuck anyone who walked away from me, and if you feel offended by my words then fuck you! I don't have all the answers and I am sure I never will, but I am on a mission to find out all that I can.

Quest,
Cornell Hurley

That he had found it did not
Necessarily mean it had been lost.
    Richard Perry

THE CONCRETE JUNGLE BEARS NO SHADE

13 Feb 21

Since I can recall I've been searching. I've been on a mission seeking to discover something. I desperately want to discover who I am, what I'm meant to be, and to know if I will be one of the greats. Today I write from a prison cell, not allowing where I am to hinder me. Incarcerated but yet free in my mind, my attitude today is fuck it! Fuck you to, fuck anyone who may have doubted me, fuck anyone who walked away from me, and if you feel offended by my words then Fuck You! I don't have all the answers and I am sure I never will but I am on a mission to find out all that I can.

Quest,

That he had found it did not
necessarily mean it had been lost.
— Richard Perry —

CORNELL HURLEY JR.

Come Home
Come home to me
A Pharoah you will be
Not a King
Come home to me
No longer will you purchase
The finer things in life
Rubies and diamonds
Are within me
Come home to me
Listen to stories
You would have never known
Come home to me
Roam the Garden of Eden freely
And eat of any tree
Come home to me
I miss you dearly
And need you next to me
Come home to me
If you truly
Desire to be free
I am the Motherland
I've given birth
To every woman and man
Come home to me
So that you
May live again
Come home to me
Sincerely,
Africa

THE CONCRETE JUNGLE BEARS NO SHADE

Come Home

Come home to me
a Pharaoh you will be
not a King

Come home to me
no longer will you purchase
the finer things in life
rubies and diamonds
are within me

Come home to me
listen to stories
you would have never known

Come home to me
roam the Garden of Eden freely
an eat of any tree

Come home to me
I miss you dearly
and need you next to me

Come home to me
if you truly
desire to be free

I am the mother land
I've given birth
to every woman & man

Come home to me
so that you
may live again

Come home to me

Sincerely,
Africa

CORNELL HURLEY JR.

14 Feb 21

Looking out at the night sky from the top floor I feel inspired. I know that I will receive all of the blessings that await me. No longer will I allow people to straddle the fence. You're either with me or against me. If you aren't helping you can only be standing in the way. Too many years have been taken from me and now I feel as if I have nothing left to give. Anything that is taken from beyond this point is going to come with a hell of a price. A single minute of my time is now too much to spare. So know that I mean it when I say get bitches get money and everything that may come along with it. Put the money first and the rest will follow $.

I'm serious,
Cornell Hurley

I'll probably never know how love feels because everything I gave my heart to ain't with me now like it wasn't real.
    Derez De'Shon

THE CONCRETE JUNGLE BEARS NO SHADE

14 Feb 21

Looking out at the night sky from the top floor, I feel inspired. I know that I will receive all of the blessings that await me. No longer will I allow people to straddle the fence. You're either with me or against me. If you aren't helping you can only be standing in the way. So many years have been taken from me and now I feel as if I have nothing left to give. Anything that is taken from beyond this point is going to come with a hell of a price. A single minute of my time is now to much to spare. Jo know that I mean it when I say get bitches get money and everything that may come along with it. Get the money first and the rest will follow $

I'm serious

I'll probably never know how love feels, because everything I gave my heart to went with me now like it wouldn't last. — Dowz De' Shon —

9 March 21

The system continues to fuck over people day in and day out. I have been a victim numerous amounts of times. I've stayed quiet for far too long, no longer will I stand by and fall victim to the system created by the S.A.C. Follow in my footsteps or lay down for the man. Stop all that fucking complaining, get a plan to implement change. Stand firm before our enemy and go hard for your family, friends, culture, rights, and skin tone no matter how dark or light. Be Black!

Salam,

Cornell Hurley

Change your mind and you will change your life. Usually what we travel miles to see is closer than we think.

    Traditional

THE CONCRETE JUNGLE BEARS NO SHADE

9 March 21

The system continues to fuck over people day in and day out. I have been a victim numerous amounts of times. I've stayed quiet for far to long, no longer will I stand by and fall victim to the system created by the S.H.C. Follow in my foot steps or lay down for the man. Stop all that fucking complaining, get a plan to implement change. Stand firm before our enemy and go hard for your family, friends, culture, rights, and skin tone no matter how dark or light. Be Black!

Selżm

Change your mind, and you will change your life. Usually what we travel miles to see is closer than we think.
— Traditional —

19 March 21

The feeling of loving someone you are not supposed to love. I pray that you never know it. There is a great deal of pain involved. The one you love may be closer to you than family but yet somehow so far away. Watching them search for a romance that could last forever, knowing that if they are to find love it will surely fade away hurts more day by day. The love they desperately search for, I know I am capable of giving. However, life has a set of rules for every game which we choose to play and the game of love is no different so there are rules we must follow. If only there was a place where the rules we could bend, I would have you as my woman and I'd be your man. Until then…

Love is like a virus. It can happen to anyone at any time.
    Maya Angelou

THE CONCRETE JUNGLE BEARS NO SHADE

19 March 21

The feeling of loving someone you are not suppose to love. I pray that you never know it. There is a great deal of pain involved. The one you love may be closer to you than family but yet somehow so far away. Watching them search for a romance that could last forever, knowing that if they are to find love it will surely fade away hurts more day by day. The love they desprotely search for, I know I am capable of giving. However, life has a set of rules for every game which we choose to play and the game of love is no different so there are rules we must follow. If only there was a place where the rules we could bend, I would have you as my woman and I'd be your man. Until then.....

Love is like a virus. It can happen to anyone at anytime.
— Maya Angelou —

CORNELL HURLEY JR.

25 March 21

Shit, I can't even get a good night of rest for thinking about you. Thinking about us and what we could have been. I often pray that there would be no need for that question again. Instead maybe I should be asking what are we going to be? Deep down inside I just don't feel like it's over yet. I don't know why I still believe in you or why I still believe in love, but I do. You introduced my heart to love and now I just cannot go on without you. No matter how sad I may get, no matter how much I may hurt, to you I will remain as faithful as a puppy. I cross my heart I will never let you down. Whenever you're done doing whatever it is that you're doing, I'll be right here waiting for you. I will always be around for another round of your love.

I don't wanna forget the present is a gift and I don't wanna take for granted the time you may have here with me.
    Alicia Keys

THE CONCRETE JUNGLE BEARS NO SHADE

12:20 a.m

25 March 21

Shit, I can't even get a good night of rest, for thinking about you thinking about us and what we could have been. I often pray that there would be no need for that question again. Instead maybe I should be asking what are we going to be? Deep down inside I just don't feel like it's over yet. I don't know why I still believe in you, or why I still believe in love but I do. You introduced my heart to love and now I just cannot go on without you. No matter how sad I may get, no matter how much I may hurt, to you I will remain as faithful as a puppy. I cross my heart I will never let you down. Whenever, your done doing whatever it is that you're doing, I'll be right here waiting for you. I will always be around for another round of your love.

    I don't wanna forget the presence
    as a gift and I don't wanna take
    for granted the time you may have here
      with me.
    — Alicia Keys —

CORNELL HURLEY JR.

26 March 21

None of us are responsible for our birth. Our responsibility is the use we make of life.
    Zora Neale Hurston

My son not only today but everyday I'm alive, I wish nothing but the best for you. You have given me a reason to continue living during a time I consider to be my lowest. Baby boy, you are not only a gift to God's earth but a gift to me as well. Even on your birthday there is nothing I could ever give you to repay you for all the joy and hope you've given me. Happy sixth birthday C3.
  Love popz,
  Cornell Hurley

THE CONCRETE JUNGLE BEARS NO SHADE

26 March 21

None of us are responsible for our birth.
Our responsibility is the use we make of life.
— Zora Neale Hurston —

My son not only today but everyday I'm alive, I wish nothing but the best for you. You have given me a reason to continue living, during a time I consider to be my lowest. Baby boy you are not only a gift to God's earth but a gift to me as well. Even on your birthday there is nothing I could ever give you, to repay you for all the joy and hope you've given me. Happy sixth birthday C3.

Love popz

CORNELL HURLEY JR.

What's a gal to do
When you've been gone
Far too long
Whether you were
After the mighty dollar
Working night and day
When you've been gone
Far too long
A house is no longer a home
What good is a table
To her
With no mouth to feed
What good is the daily paper
Without you there to read
What good is a bed
When the headboard
No longer rocks
When you been gone
Far too long
Jodi will knock
So hurry home
Before that itch
Needs a scratch
Before you know it
She'll be on her back
Caress her
Like a stack of money
You've worked for
Clean your plate
Eat everything
Until she's through
Afterwards let her
Lick your fingers clean
Place a pillow
Behind the headboard
Drowning out the sound
And when Jodi
Come snooping around

THE CONCRETE JUNGLE BEARS NO SHADE

Make sure he
Hears you
Beatin' that pussy down!

*What's a gal to do
when you've been gone
far to long
Whether you were
after the mighty dollar
working night and day
When you've been gone
far to long
a house is no longer a home
What good is a table
to her
with no mouth to feed
What good is the daily paper
without you there to read
What good is a bed
when the headboard
no longer rocks
When you been gone
far to long
Jodi will knock
So hurry home
before that itch
needs a scratch
before you know it
she'll be on her back
Caress her
like a stack of money
you've worked for
Clean your plate
eat everything
until she's through
afterwards let her
lick your fingers clean
Place a pillow
behind the headboard
drawing out the sound
and when Jodi
come snooping around
make sure he
hears you
beatin that pussy down!*

Ha!

CORNELL HURLEY JR.

He was against all change, except the kind he jingled in his pocket.
William Hastie

Nothing in life is constant but change. Especially people, people constantly change. Currently I am in the process of training my heart to be let down over and over again. Call me negative but I will always have a shoulder for you to cry on when you realize that the person you gave your heart to has changed. The only logic you may depend on throughout your life is that nothing or no one will ever stay the same. People no matter who they are will always change. Even as I stare in the mirror, I notice change.
Constantly,
Cornell Hurley

THE CONCRETE JUNGLE BEARS NO SHADE

27 March 21

> He was against all change, except
> the kind he jingled in his pocket.
> — William Hastie —

Nothing in life is constant but change. Especially people, people constantly change. Currently I am in the process of training my heart to be let down, over and over again. Call me negative but I will always have a shoulder for you to cry on, when you realize that the person you gave your heart to has changed. The only logic you may depend on throughout your life is that nothing or no one will ever stay the same. People no matter who they are will always change. Even as I stare in the mirror, I notice change.

Constantly,

CORNELL HURLEY JR.

Some males seem to think the amount of time in which they've lived makes them men. Contrary to what most males may think, what separates boys from men is not how much time you've been around but how have you made that time serve you. Finding ways in which you can have time serve you is no easy task. Truth is we all have the power to decide what we're going to do with our time. Boys decide to do whatever it is they'd like to do with their time, while men on the other hand spend their time doing what must be done in order to survive.

Don't think because you've been surviving just simply getting by that you're a man. Are you living the life you've always wanted to live? If not you're doing what must be done to come closer to living that ideal lifestyle. Time is of the essence. Let's grow into men.

Time can be your enemy or your friend.
Ray Charles

THE CONCRETE JUNGLE BEARS NO SHADE

2 April 21

Some males seem to think the amount of time in which they've lived makes them men. Contrary to what most males may think, what seperates boys from men is not how much time you've been around but how have you made that time serve you. Finding ways in which you can have time serve you is no easy task. Truth is we all have the power to decide what we're going to do with our time. Boys decide to do whatever it is they'd like to do with their time, while men on the other hand spend their time doing what must be done in order to survive.

Don't think because you've been surviving, just simply getting by that you're a man. Are you living the life you've always wanted to live? If not your doing what must be done to come closer to living that idea lifestyle? Time is of the essence. Let's grow into men.

Time can be your enemy or your friend.
— Ray Charles

7 April 21 12:15 a.m.

No zzzz…

To live in the midst of learning, what a struggle. I imagine what my life may be like if I knew all that I didn't know. Probably wouldn't make any difference seeing how I've learned many lessons from my past over and over again, following my heart instead of being guided by my knowledge of what was and what has been. I have begun to lose faith in humanity. Everyone seems to be selfish when it comes to others. If I learned from the past I wouldn't be asking questions of myself. Why do I still care?

I am desperately trying not to give a fuck. I had no idea how hard it could be. 38

Headaches,
Cornell Hurley

THE CONCRETE JUNGLE BEARS NO SHADE

R30   ZZZZZZ....

7 ~~March~~ April 21   12:15 am

    To live in the midst of learning, what a struggle. I imagine what my life may be like if I knew all that I didn't know. Probably wouldn't make any difference, seeing how I've learned many lessons from my past over and over again. Following my heart instead of being guided by my knowledge of what was and what has been. I have begun to lose faith in humanity, everyone seems to be selfish when it comes to others. If I learned from the past I wouldn't be asking questions of myself. Why do I still care?

    I am desprately trying not to give a fuck. I had no idea how hard it could be.   -38-

Headaches,

5 May 21

Life has a mission which is to challenge us all. The more we fail, life wins. It feels good when you conquer life. I cannot lose anymore. Though I bow to Allah, may life bow in front of me. What I desire I will have.

Living,

Cornell Hurley

THE CONCRETE JUNGLE BEARS NO SHADE

5 May 21

Life has a mission which is to challenge us all. The more we fail life wins. It feels good when you concure life. I can not lose anymore. Though I bow to Allah, may life bow in front of me. What I desire I will have.

Living,

24 April 21

Though I am eager to know what it may feel like to give my all to a cause, whenever I try to commit I fall short. At times I feel as if what I am asking is too much of life but how am I to truly know if I cannot commit. Time I feel is running out. If I must start now, the question then becomes where the fuck do I start?

To act is to be committed, and to be committed is to be in danger.
James Baldwin

THE CONCRETE JUNGLE BEARS NO SHADE

24 April 21

Though I am eager to know what it may feel like to give my all to a cause, whenever, I try to commit I fall short. At times I feel as if what I am asking is too much of life but how am I to truly know if I cannot commit. Time I feel is running out. If I must start now, the question then becomes where the fuck do I start?

> To act is to be
> committed, and to be
> committed is to be in
> danger.
> — James Baldwin —

8 May 21

Can you imagine envying the one you love. Though you may not value your day-to-day life, I do. If I was given the chance to trade places with you, within a split second I wouldn't think twice about it. I hold you to a higher standard than I do most simply because you mean the world to me. However, due to my incarceration far beyond your flaws I now see. The truth has been exposed and I now know that you don't believe in love as much as me. You need it to be physical but in order to truly be in love, you should know it's about more than physical touch and the distance between us. Honestly, I just don't understand how no one can love as hard as me. Loving you from within my cell is good enough for me. Unfortunately, love isn't only about me and it's for that reason alone friends we will always be.

Lexus,
Cornell Hurley

THE CONCRETE JUNGLE BEARS NO SHADE

8 May 21

Can you imagine envying the one you love. Though you may not value your day to day life, I do. If I was given the chance to trade places with you, within a split second I wouldn't think twice about it. I hold you to a higher standard than I do most, simply because you mean the world to me. However, due to my incarceration far beyond your flaws I now see. The truth has been exposed and I now know that you don't believe in love as much as me. You need it to be physical but in order to truly be in love, you should know it's about more than physical touch and the distance between us. Honestly, I just don't understand how no one can love as hard as me. Loving you from within my cell is good enough for me. Unfortunately, love isn't only about me and it's for that reason alone, friends we will always be.

Lexus,

13 May 21

Up early 3 a.m. getting to the money. It's more than abs, arms, back, and legs. You will see dedication when you look at me. Fuck, I owe it to myself. I am somebody. Grind hard!

THE CONCRETE JUNGLE BEARS NO SHADE

13 May 21

Up early 3 am getting to the money. It's more than abs, arms, back, and legs. You will see dedication when you look at me. Fuck, I owe it to myself. I am somebody. Grind hard!

6 June 21

The goal is to no longer communicate for shits and giggles but to become more efficient at public speaking. No longer will I chase popularity by having a large quantity of friends, but one good friend will do me just fine. A great follower I've been for far too long. No longer will I make my sole mission to help others reach their dreams while neglecting my own. When success is the only option, you must ask more of yourself. I know that I am beyond average, I am the image of pure excellence.

To be successful, grow to the point where one completely forgets himself, that is to lose himself in a great cause.
    Booker T. Washington

6 June 21

The goal is to no longer communicate for shits and giggles but to become more efficient at public speaking. No longer will I chase popularity by having a large quantity of friends but one good friend will do me just fine. A great follower I've been for far to long, no longer will I make my soul mission to help others reach their dreams while neglecting my own. When success is the only option, you must ask more of yourself. I know that I am beyond average, I am the image of pure excellence.

> "To be successful, grow to the point where one completely forgets himself, that is to lose himself in a great cause."
> Booker T. Washington

18 Aug 21

Can you see past all of my insecurities. Though I stare deep into your eyes can you see that I'd rather bury my head and hide. Through my display of anger can you tell that I am truly afraid, afraid of loving. When I love, I love hard in hopes of receiving if only a fraction back. Can you see that I love you simply because of my insecurities and I'd rather you not feel like me. Can you see? Truth be told if anyone could I thought that it would be you to see the best in me. Tell me what is it that you see?

THE CONCRETE JUNGLE BEARS NO SHADE

18 Aug 21

Can you see past all of my insecurities. Though I stare deep into your eyes can you see that I'd rather burry my head and hide. Through my display of anger can you tell that I am truly afraid, afraid of loving. When I love, I love hard in hopes of recieving if only a fraction back. Can you see that I love you simply because of my insecurities and I'd rather you not feel like me. Can you see? Truth be told if anyone could I thought that it would be you to see the best in me. Tell me what is it that you see?

21 Aug 21

The more I write, I'm finding it to be quite hard to speak my truth. From the top of the mountain, my story will be told. The world must know my story, who I am, where I've been, and all that I've done. If the world is to know my story, then they will soon know of you. For my story would be incomplete without you. With love is where my story begins, and once love can be no more is where my story shall end.

Fucking Love,

38

THE CONCRETE JUNGLE BEARS NO SHADE

21 Aug 21

The more I write, I'm finding it to be quite hard to speak my truth. From the top of the mountain, my story will be told. The world must know my story, who I am, where I've been and all that I've done. If the world is to know my story, then they will soon know of you. For my story would be incomplete without you.

With love is where my story begins and once love can be no more is where my story shall end.

Fucking Love
S8

7,

In the midst of The Concrete Jungle I met a character unlike any character I'd met before. When this character spoke its words were always felt. This character had a way of pulling me away from my personal story and causing me to focus on their story. An attempt to describe the beauty of this character would be strenuous, so I won't attempt to do such. This character once told a story of an author who lived in a fairytale but could not be the author of his own story.

The author in which the character spoke of was known not to accept defeat. The author was known to not live in a world of reality. Everything the author had encountered in his life he perceived as a challenge. Even the introduction of this new character who challenged his belief he perceived as nothing more than a challenge. Desperately he attempted to capture the heart of this character. The author refused to take into consideration the limitations that The Concrete Jungle would have on his dream. The author thought through spoken word or written that he could obtain that in which he truly desired. He was wrong. That author is now learning to live with reality, to accept that life will not always be pliable to all that he may desire and most importantly the author now knows that he cannot write a perfect script 4 his life, let alone write himself into the story of someone else.

In ending, meeting you was bittersweet because you gave me something to lose. Something that I will carry with me until The Concrete Jungle bears shade.

Sincerely,

38 The Author

7.

In the midst of The Concrete Jungle I met a character unlike any character I'd met before. When this character spoke it's words were always ♥ felt. This character had a way of pulling me away from my personal story and causing me to focus on their story. An attempt to describe the beauty of this character would be strenuous, so I won't attempt to do such. This character once told a story of an author who lived in a fairytale but could not be the author of his own story.

The author in which the character spoke of was known not to accept defeat. The author was known to not live in a world of reality. Everything the author had encountered in his life he perceived as a challenge. Even the introduction of this new character who challenged his belief he perceived as nothing more than a challenge, desperately he attempted to capture the heart of this character. The author refused to take into consideration the limitations that the Concrete Jungle would have on his dream. The author thought through spoken word or written

CORNELL HURLEY JR.

that he could obtain that in which he truly desired. He was wrong. That author is now learning to live with reality, to accept that life will not always be pliable to all that he may desire, and most importantly the author now knows that he cannot write a perfect script 4 his life - yet alone write himself into the story of someone else.

In *Ending*, meeting you was bitter sweet. Because you gave me something to lose. Something that I will carry with me until the Concrete Jungle bones shade.

Sincerely,
The Author

CPSIA information can be obtained
at www.ICGtesting.com
Printed in the USA
BVHW081115240722
642887BV00012B/1067